by
Clare Oliver

Perilous Pest
Although the tiny mosquito doesn't look very fierce, it kills more people in a year than any other creature.

TIGER TERROR

The tiger is a huge cat, hunting alone in jungle and rough country across southern and eastern Asia. Usually, it feasts on deer and wild pigs - although one tiger in the Himalayas ate 438 people in 8 years in the early 1900s!

FIERCE QUIZ

Which of these is not a real kind of tiger?
a) Chinese
b) Hawaiian
c) Sumatran

What markings does a leopard have on its coat?
a) stripes
b) diamonds
c) spots

How many tigers are there in the wild?
a) less than 10,000
b) 50,000
c) over 200,000

(answers on page 32)

WATCH OUT, RUDOLPH!

The only big cat left in Europe is the European lynx, a solitary hunter of deer in the snowy woodlands of eastern and northern Europe. At around a metre in length, this largest member of the lynx family sneaks up on roe deer or reindeer at night, suffocating them with a bite to the throat.

Leopard

TREE-TOP TREATS

The leopard, a slightly smaller cousin of the tiger, has found a way to prevent jackals and other scavengers from making off with its left-overs. After a feast, it can drag the carcass up into the branches of a tree, keeping a tasty snack for later.

2

TABBIES & TIGERS

Tigers might look a bit like domestic cats, but at six times longer they are not lap-cat material.

TWO-FACED

Tigers will attack people, especially if the tigers are elderly and find it hard to catch enough food, or if they are raising cubs in places where food is scarce. Tigers prefer to pounce from behind, so some Indian villagers living near tiger reserves wear fake 'faces' on the back of their heads.

Bengal tiger

MONSTER MOGGIE

The biggest cat in the world is the Siberian tiger, of northern China and Russia. Weighing up to a massive 290 kg, with a shoulder height of 1 metre, the Siberian tiger is a match for any animal. Some tigers will even have a bash at killing elephants!

STRENGTH IN NUMBERS

Chapman's zebra

Lions must be the most sociable of the big cats, as they live in groups and hunt in teams. Together, a group of lionesses sneak up on a herd of buffalo or zebra and surround them. At the right moment, one or two deliberately panic the prey, to trick them into running straight at their sister hunters, hidden in the long grass.

LION'S SHARE

Adult male lions do very little hunting, though they will claim first bite at any prey the females have killed. The males can eat up to 35 kg of meat at once – about the same as a ten-year-old boy would weigh. Males spend most of their time defending their territory and family from other males.

Lion attack

ON THE MENU

Lions typically hunt grazing animals such as zebra, wildebeest, antelope and gazelle. But they don't mind taking a mouthful of a baboon or an African hunting dog. If they're really hungry, they might also sink a tooth into a big buffalo, a human, or even a hippopotamus.

CHEW CHEW!

Building work on one of Africa's first railways had to be stopped when a pair of lions took to feasting on the railway workers by night. World-famous marksmen had to be brought in to find and kill these rogue lions before the work could be completed.

GREEDY GUTS

Lions in zoos have been known to try to eat other zoo animals – including hippos!

KRUGER KILLERS

Lions in South Africa's Kruger National Park have developed a taste for human flesh, hunting out illegal immigrants who attempt to cross the park on foot from Mozambique. Once a pride discovers that humans are easy meat, no one is safe. Rangers had to put down five man-eaters in 1997.

FIERCE QUIZ

For how long might a lion laze about after a good meal?

a) 1 day
b) 3 days
c) 1 week

Where did the ancient Romans find lions for their circuses?

a) Greece
b) Palestine
c) Egypt

How many lions are there in the average pride?

a) 5
b) 15
c) 50

(answers on page 32)

HOWLING WOLF

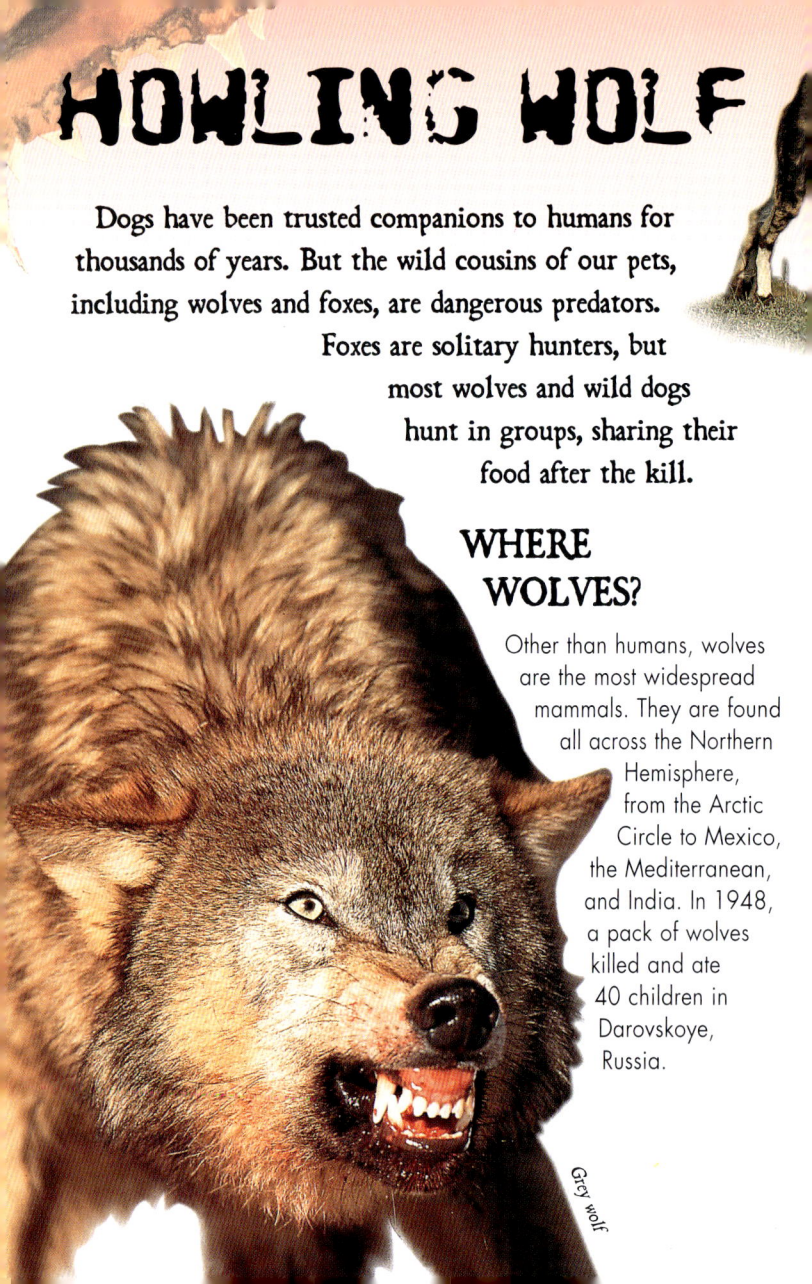

Dogs have been trusted companions to humans for thousands of years. But the wild cousins of our pets, including wolves and foxes, are dangerous predators. Foxes are solitary hunters, but most wolves and wild dogs hunt in groups, sharing their food after the kill.

WHERE WOLVES?

Other than humans, wolves are the most widespread mammals. They are found all across the Northern Hemisphere, from the Arctic Circle to Mexico, the Mediterranean, and India. In 1948, a pack of wolves killed and ate 40 children in Darovskoye, Russia.

Grey wolf

CAPE CRUSADER

The African hunting dog, living in southern Africa, is a real menace. Also known as the Cape hunting dog, it hunts by day in packs up to 60-strong, making up for its smaller size by moving fast and overwhelming bigger animals by sheer numbers.

Wild dogs

GIVE A DOG A BONE

Grey wolf packs might number over 20 animals. Hunting together at night, a pack of wolves will eat anything from insects up to musk oxen and deer. They are normally scared of humans, but not always! Stalking herds of large herbivores, the pack singles out stragglers and chases them down, leaving only hair and bones behind.

WILY COYOTE

The coyote is craftier than its larger cousin, the wolf. Hunting rodents and rabbits by night, and gobbling up any carrion or rubbish it can find, the coyote gives urban America the shivers with its nightly yips and howls. American Indians celebrate the coyote's crafty behaviour and greediness in hundreds of folk tales.

FIERCE QUIZ

How much does a male grey wolf weigh?
a) 35–45 kg
b) 70–80 kg
c) half a tonne

How fast can a coyote sprint?
a) 30 km/h
b) 50 km/h
c) 64 km/h

How many toes does the African hunting dog have on each front paw?
a) 3
b) 4
c) 5

(answers on page 32)

GREAT & SMALL
The largest wild dog is the grey wolf – it's four times longer than the smallest, the fennec fox.

MOTOR-MOUTH

Shrews are hyperactive hunters, with special hook-tipped fangs for grabbing slippery prey, such as worms and small fish. Many are expert swimmers, but they hunt on land too, for insects and other small prey – they even hunt each other! The Etruscan shrew has to eat three times its own body weight every day just to stay alive.

HOW SWEET!

The Etruscan shrew is truly tiny, weighing about as much as a sugar lump.

Cape clawless otter

POISON DWARF

The American short-tailed shrew is one of only a very few mammals to use poison. This shrew has special saliva which is toxic enough to kill small fish and frogs. In the unlikely event that this shrew bit a person, it wouldn't be fatal – it's too small for that.

Shrew

NOT SO CUTE!

Small furry animals are often more dangerous than they appear. Tiny shrews and playful otters might make us want to stroke them, but in the wild they can be every bit as fearsome as lions and tigers.

OTTER-LY HUGE!

The giant African (or Cape clawless) otter can grow up to a whopping 1 metre long, not counting the tail, but it's still not the biggest otter in the world. It has a giant cousin in Brazil which grows up to 1.5 metres long, plus a 0.7-metre tail.

ALL AT SEA

Although they can run faster than people, otters of all types are most at home underwater, where their webbed feet and powerful tails can carry them almost half a kilometre without surfacing for air. They hunt fish, frogs – and anything else that moves! Even shellfish aren't safe from some seafaring otters, which carry stones to smash the seashells open.

FIERCE QUIZ

Where do freshwater otters go to sleep?
a) in a tree
b) in a burrow
c) on lily pads

What's the quickest way to kill a nervous shrew?
a) make a loud noise
b) tickle it
c) feed it cheese

How big is the biggest shrew?
a) 2 cm
b) 37 cm
c) 1 metre

(answers on page 32)

DASTARDLY DRAGON

There is a dragon lurking in Indonesia. It's called a Komodo dragon and is actually a lizard which can grow as long as a car, weigh up to 130 kg, and live for 100 years. You wouldn't want to investigate this dragon's burrow to see if it's guarding treasure!

Gila monster

OPEN WIDE!

When you're as big as a car, you need a mouth the size of a dinner plate to fuel up!

MEXICAN MONSTER

Gila (pronounced 'heela') monsters roam the deserts of Mexico and the southwestern United States at night, hunting small mammals, birds and bird eggs. When this lizard bites you, it just won't let go. The poisonous bite can affect your heart and breathing, and can even kill.

10

COOL CUSTOMER

The Gila monster is unusual for a cold-blooded animal, as it hunts only at night. Lizards usually rely on the sun to warm them up and get them going. Part of the Gila monster's secret is its fatty tail. By storing fat during warm summer nights, it doesn't need to hunt when it's cold.

NICE TO MEAT YOU

Komodo dragons are not very nice to each other. Finding a mate is a tricky business, because the dragons are just as likely to eat each other as make friends. Newly-hatched Komodo dragons, about 45 cm long, take to the trees until they've grown a bit – probably to avoid the hungry adults!

SMELLY BREATH

Komodo dragons have been known to hunt large mammals, and even people, but they prefer to feast on smelly carrion and small animals. Though it isn't poisonous, the Komodo dragon's dental hygiene is so bad that one bite can infect you with all kinds of nasty germs.

Komodo dragon

FIERCE QUIZ

How deep can the Komodo dragon burrow?

a) 2 metres
b) 5 metres
c) 9 metres

What does the Gila monster's Latin name, *Heloderma*, mean?

a) funny feet
b) bead-like scales
c) spotty face

Apart from the Gila monster, what other lizard is venomous?

a) Mexican beaded lizard
b) Scottish kilted lizard
c) Godzilla

(answers on page 32)

MAN-EATER

The saltwater crocodile is the biggest reptile on Earth and the scariest! It eats more people each year than any other carnivore. The biggest salties grow to over 10 metres long, though most are only about half that length. Whatever the size, it has a massive appetite. It has the power to drag buffalo and cattle down and then its razor-sharp teeth provide the tools to finish the job.

SWAMP OF DEATH

The worst-ever carnage by crocodiles was reported in World War II. About 1,000 Japanese soldiers were cornered by the British in a mangrove swamp off the coast of Burma (now Myanmar). After both sides settled down for the night, the British heard terrible screams and gunshots from across the swamp. Tempted by the bloody smells of battle, local crocodiles had moved in for a feast. By the morning, only 20 Japanese soldiers were still alive.

TERRIBLE CROCODILES

75 million years ago, the swamps and lakes of what is now Texas were home to the Terrible crocodile. Scientists reckon this monster croc was the longest predator ever: its skull alone was over 2 metres long – big enough for a man to fit lengthways in its mouth with space to spare. Yikes!

FIERCE QUIZ

How many people does the saltwater crocodile eat each year?
a) 25
b) 500
c) 2,000

How many of the 22 species in the crocodile family are known to eat people?
a) 2
b) 5
c) 7

In the 1860s, a Nile crocodile grabbed a very unlikely prey. Was it:
a) an elephant?
b) a domestic cat?
c) a bearded vulture?

(answers on page 32)

SNEAKY SNAPPERS

SNAP!

A river hunter must keep low in the water so that its prey doesn't see it. The crocodile weighs itself down with up to 13 kg of stones and pebbles until just its snout is above the surface!

A 1-tonne crocodile has 13 tonnes-worth of crushing power in its jaws. That's 26 times stronger than you can bite. Even so, the muscles that open the jaws are so weak that an elastic band could hold a 2-metre-long crocodile's mouth shut!

NEVER SMILE AT A CROCODILE

Just a bit smaller than its cousin the saltie, the Nile crocodile is another vicious predator. One that was shot in Botswana in 1969 contained some gruesome remains in its stomach: a zebra, a donkey, two goats and a partly-digested woman.

Nile crocodile

FIERCE FISH

There are some deadly predators below water in some rivers and seas. In South American rivers, schools of razor-toothed piranha fish can strip a victim of its flesh in minutes. In warm seas, an even scarier menace preys upon seafaring animals and humans - the shark!

SUPER SENSE

A shark can pick up the scent of one part blood in 100 million parts water.

Great white shark

TOOTHY GRIN

One of the scariest things about sharks is their toothy grin. Sharks can have thousands of teeth, in several rows. With all its biting and tearing at potential food, a shark gets through a set of teeth very quickly. But it constantly has new sets of teeth growing behind, to replace the old or broken ones.

NASTY NIP

A close look at a piranha's mouth shows just how well-adapted they are for nibbling larger creatures to death. Mounted in a very powerful jaw, the piranha's teeth are razor-sharp triangles which snip shut around a mouthful of flesh like a pair of scissors.

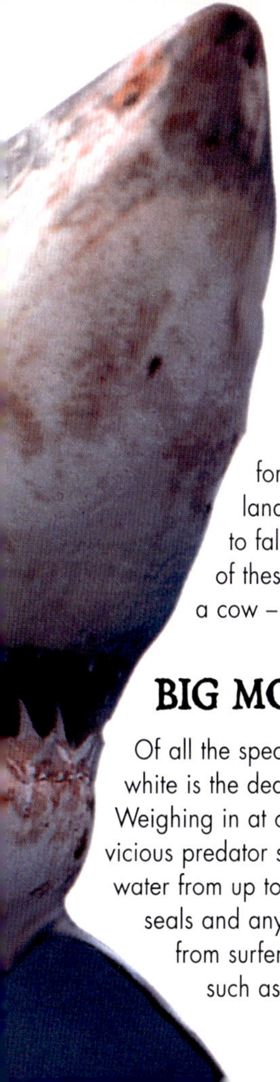

Black piranha (Cannibal fish)

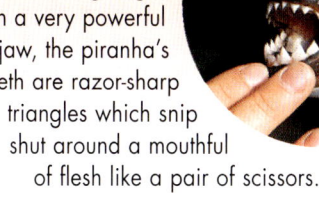

SNAPPY SWIMMERS

Piranhas are mainly freshwater fish, which eat any old meat they discover, and hunt other fish. They are notorious for their eagerness to attack land animals unlucky enough to fall into their river. A school of these plate-sized fish can eat a cow – or a human – in minutes.

BIG MOUTH

Of all the species of shark, the great white is the deadliest to humans. Weighing in at over 2.5 tonnes, this vicious predator senses movement in water from up to 1.5 km away. It grabs seals and anything vaguely similar, from surfers to indigestible rubbish such as old car tyres.

FIERCE QUIZ

Which of these has not been found in a shark's stomach?

a) car numberplate
b) suit of armour
c) ship's anchor

How long is a great white shark?

a) 3 metres
b) 10 metres
c) 15 metres

Up to how big can a piranha grow?

a) 20 cm
b) 60 cm
c) 5 metres

(answers on page 32)

AMPHIBIAN ASSASSINS

Poison-arrow frog

Poisonous frogs and toads really only use their poisons to make larger hunters spit them out when they're mistaken for dinner. But some frogs are so poisonous that people in the South American rainforests have learnt to use them to be better predators themselves. A single poison-arrow frog carries enough poison to make 1,000 deadly arrows or blow-darts.

FIERCE QUIZ

If you're bitten by a poisonous snake you should...
a) bite it back
b) send for the antidote
c) jump up and down saying 'Ow!'

In which of these places would you be safe from wild cobras?
a) Brazil
b) Africa
c) India

Where does the female poison-arrow frog lay her eggs?
a) on a leaf
b) on her mate's back
c) in a puddle

(answers on page 32)

SERPENTS OF THE SEAS

Snakes that live in the sea can be a hundred times more poisonous than any land snake. Luckily for fishermen and swimmers, sea snakes are not keen on biting humans. Unfortunately, though, when they do bite, it can be completely painless – so you don't know you've been bitten until the poison starts working.

SPIT ON!

Spitting cobras can successfully hit a target up to 3 metres away.

16

DEADLY POISON

Snakes and frogs are natural experts at using poisons. The viper family of snakes has long fangs on hinges, which unfold from the roof of the mouth when the viper bites, injecting venom into its prey. Many vipers, including the rattlesnake, can hunt in pitch darkness, homing in on their victim's body heat.

PRIME POISONER

The king cobra is the world's largest venomous snake, with one specimen measuring 5.5 metres. As with other cobras, it rears up and spreads a 'hood' when threatened. Its venom is poisonous enough to kill an elephant, but it mainly hunts other snakes.

BULLS-EYE!

Deadly spitting cobras don't have to get close to poison you. They can 'spit' venom from the special pouches in their mouths, aiming for the eyes of their victims. Some snake-hunters wear shiny baubles around their necks, so that if a cobra spits at them, it will aim at the wrong part of their body.

Cobra

FANCY A GAME OF SQUASH?

It is very rare that a python attempts to give a human a hug, but it has been known to happen. In 1979, a young herdsman in South Africa was grabbed by a 4.5-metre African rock python. When help arrived 20 minutes later, the man had been suffocated – and swallowed whole.

FIERCE QUIZ

How long was the longest python ever measured?

a) 6 metres
b) 8 metres
c) 10 metres

How heavy was the biggest giant anaconda ever caught?

a) 110 kg
b) 225 kg
c) 500 kg

What's the biggest snake meal ever recorded?

a) 35-kg child
b) 59-kg impala
c) 10-tonne rhino

(answers on page 32)

FEATHER BOAS

The boa constrictor has a habit of crushing the life out of its victims. Some boas are equipped with heat sensors for hunting in darkness. Although many lurk in rivers and ponds, some are arboreal (living in trees) and have especially long teeth to help them snap up unlucky birds.

PIGGING OUT

The giant anaconda is the grand-daddy of all the suffocating serpents. Usually a mere 5 metres long, but thought to grow up to a terrifying 10 metres, this water-loving monster thinks nothing of strangling pigs and caimans (a sort of alligator) for breakfast. After biting and suffocating them, it swallows them whole, and takes a well-earned rest.

TALL TALES

The giraffe may be the tallest animal in Africa, but the reticulated python is the longest!

SQUASHED TO DEATH

Bull python

Some snakes don't need to poison their prey to kill it – they just give it a big hug instead. Boas, pythons and anacondas live all across the tropics, from South America to China, hunting anything from mice and rats to goats, pigs and deer. Only the very largest ones ever consider squeezing humans to death.

Diamond python

MASTER MOUSER

Pythons are very effective rat-catchers. They are welcomed in some villages as a good alternative to a cat for controlling vermin. But their larger cousins would happily make off with the villagers' pigs and goats – and are less popular!

OCEAN KILLERS

Sharks may be the fiercest fish in the world, but the oceans are stalked by another dangerous predator - the killer whale. Travelling in family groups, or pods, up to 40-strong, killer whales can cause panic among the penguin and seal populations of Arctic ice floes as they arrive for a feast.

WATER WOLVES

Working as a group, like a pack of very big wolves, killer whales have been known to attack young blue whales, the biggest animal in the world.
They can slice through the water at incredible speed, enabling them to surprise groups of seals and penguins and snap up the stragglers.

Killer whale

LAND LUBBERS

Along the shores of Patagonia, South America, killer whales sometimes pay a surprise visit to the clusters of sea-lions and pups on the beach by riding up onto the beach like surfers! When they successfully grab a sea-lion, they take it out to sea and play with it, like a cat with a mouse, before eating it.

FIN-TASTIC FACT

The dorsal fin of a killer whale reaches 1.8 metres – as tall as a grown man!

FIERCE QUIZ

How long is a fully-grown killer whale?
a) 5 metres
b) 7 metres
c) 9 metres

What's the fastest speed a bull (male) killer whale can swim?
a) 40 km/h
b) 50 km/h
c) 55 km/h

Because shark skin is rough, it has often been used for...
a) sandpaper
b) cleaning buildings
c) non-slip bath mats

(answers on page 32)

DOLPHIN DINNERS

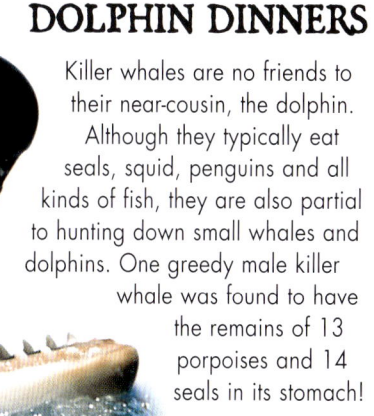

Killer whales are no friends to their near-cousin, the dolphin. Although they typically eat seals, squid, penguins and all kinds of fish, they are also partial to hunting down small whales and dolphins. One greedy male killer whale was found to have the remains of 13 porpoises and 14 seals in its stomach!

OCEAN TIGER

The closest equivalent to the killer whale in the fish kingdom is the tiger shark. Growing up to 5.5 metres long, this ferocious hunter is often found in large packs, though these are not tight-knit family groups like the whale's. It will eat anything from medium-sized fish and sea turtles to porpoises and people!

Tiger shark

ICY DESERT

Even the snowy wastelands of the Arctic are populated by ferocious hunters. King of the Arctic animal kingdom is the biggest and hungriest bear in the world. With a fondness for nice, plump seals, large polar bears are capable of stomaching 70 kg of meat at one sitting.

Polar bear and walrus

COOL CAMOUFLAGE

A dab of snow on the polar bear's black nose completes its white hunting camouflage.

MEATY MENU

The polar bear is the most carnivorous (meat-loving) of all the bear family. It is the only bear that hunts people for food. In 1995, a German tourist was eaten by a bear in the Svalbard islands, north of Norway. Polar bears will also have a go at fish, birds, caribou, walruses, and even small whales!

FATTY FEAST

Polar bears go to some lengths to hunt ringed seals, especially seal pups, whose bodies have a thick, fatty layer. In autumn, the bears may leave the meat, just eating the seal fat – they need to build up weight for their winter sleep, but the proteins in meat would make them need to keep getting up to go to the loo!

SEAL MEAL

Polar bears are incredibly good at sniffing-out a meal. Researchers in Alaska think they have found evidence of polar bears sensing the presence of seals from 64 km away! They have also been found to come running towards a whale or seal carcass from up to 32 km away.

Arctic fox

FANTASTIC FOX

At around 5 kg, the Arctic fox is about 100 times smaller than the polar bear, but often follows bears to snap-up the tasty morsels of seal they leave after a kill. The Arctic fox has special hairy feet and thick fur – these keep it perfectly comfortable in temperatures as low as -50°C.

FIERCE QUIZ

How much does a polar bear cub weigh when it's born?

a) 1 kg
b) 10 kg
c) 20 kg

How much territory does a polar bear call home?

a) 1,000 sq metres
b) 100,000 sq metres
c) 300,000 sq metres

How long is an Arctic fox?

a) 40 cm
b) 80 cm
c) 1 metre

(answers on page 32)

DEADLY TEDDY

There are probably eight species of bear (some people count the giant panda as a weird member of the racoon family). Apart from the polar bear, most bears eat a lot of plants and fruit. But all bears, including the panda, enjoy the occasional mouthful of meat, and some are very clever hunters.

SCARE BEARS

Brown bears (called grizzlies in North America) live all across the Northern Hemisphere. Alaskan brown bears are famous for their taste for salmon, which they catch by biting the fish in mid-air as they jump up waterfalls. Brown bears have also been known to kill moose, and even buffalo.

Alaskan brown bear

RUNNING WILD

A hungry brown bear can sprint at 64 km/h – that's twice as fast as a champion human sprinter. Eeek!

TEDDY TERROR

There aren't many places where you might be pursued by a bear. Some parts of Canada and northern Europe post warnings about polar bears, but attacks are very rare. Three or four people are killed every year by brown and black bears in remote parts of North America and Japan.

BEAR-LY ABSENT

Bears like to stay within their home range. Some have shown that they'll go to any lengths to get back home. In 1973, an Alaskan brown bear was taken to an island 93 km away by boat. It roamed across several islands, swimming at least 14 km in freezing water, to get back to where it was captured.

BEAR NECESSITIES

The spectacled bear enjoys a broad menu. It slurps down all sorts of fruits, berries, moss, plant bulbs, and even cacti. But it is also a hunter, taking rabbits and deer for dinner. Although it only weighs around 100 kg, this bear even dines out on cattle, unless the farmer sees it coming!

FIERCE QUIZ

How hefty was the biggest bear ever captured?

a) 800 kg
b) 900 kg
c) 1,000 kg

If you meet a big, hairy beastie in the Himalayas, it's probably...

a) the abominable snowman
b) a very lost, very cold chimp
c) a brown bear

Why do people hunt bears in Asia?

a) for ingredients for medicines
b) to make big cuddly toys
c) because they're bored

(answers on page 32)

25

DIVE-BOMBERS

FIERCE QUIZ

What does an owl do with all the bony bits of the animals it eats?
a) make soup
b) cough them up in pellets
c) wear them as jewellery

What's the fastest predator on the planet?
a) swift
b) pelican
c) peregrine falcon

How does a kestrel know where to catch a vole?
a) hears it squeak
b) sees its urine
c) asks a friend

(answers on page 32)

Some predators drop onto their prey from the skies above, taking it completely by surprise. Eagles and falcons can spot prey from a huge distance, and prefer to patrol their territory from high in the sky. Other hunting birds, such as barn owls, rely on their very sensitive ears to pinpoint their next meal.

NIGHT OWL

The barn owl is specially-equipped to hunt in almost complete darkness, seeing 100 times better than humans at night. But it could hunt with its eyes shut – this owl also has incredible hearing, picking out mice and insects in pitch darkness. To avoid deafening itself, the owl has special, soft wing feathers, for silent flying.

HOLD STEADY

Spotting prey can be tricky if you're moving around, so dive-bombing birds sometimes find a way to hover over one spot. Some simply point into the wind, using the airflow to keep them in the air. Others, such as the fish-eating pied kingfisher, flap their wings so rapidly that they become a blur, while hovering over a lake or river.

BIG BIRD

The flesh-eating condor from South America has a wingspan of up to 3 metres – the only thing with bigger wings is metal and called a plane!

EERIE EAGLE

The sea eagle can take large prey – and it's the only bird known to have carried off a human. In 1932, a little girl playing in the garden was seized by a sea eagle and dropped near its nest in the nearby mountains. She was found alive and well by a rescue team.

EAGLE EYES

Eagles, kestrels and falcons are other birds with superb vision. The golden eagle is known to spot rabbits from over 2 km away, and a peregrine falcon will chase pigeons it has spotted up to 8 km away. Since this falcon can swoop at speeds of up to 350 km/h, the chase takes less time than you might think!

CREEPY-CRAWLIES

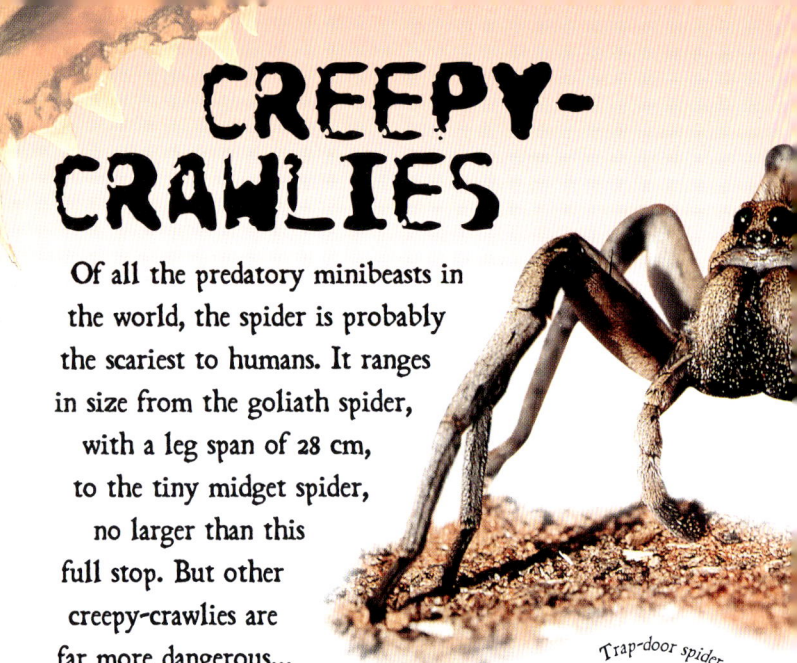

Of all the predatory minibeasts in the world, the spider is probably the scariest to humans. It ranges in size from the goliath spider, with a leg span of 28 cm, to the tiny midget spider, no larger than this full stop. But other creepy-crawlies are far more dangerous...

Trap-door spider

TOXIC FAMILY

Almost every single spider uses venomous fangs to subdue its prey. Brazilian wandering spiders, and the black widow spiders found around the world, can be deadly to humans. But most spiders reserve their venom for killing food, from other insects to mice, chickens and even small rattlesnakes!

SPIDER CHAMP

Hairy tarantulas can't kill people, but they can kill deadly rattlesnakes!

TRAP-TASTIC!

Some spiders catch their meals by just pouncing on them. But producing silk from their abdomens allows spiders to build all kinds of traps. Some make sticky webs in the air to catch flies, and even the occasional bird. Others construct traps underground, jumping out when a meal walks past.

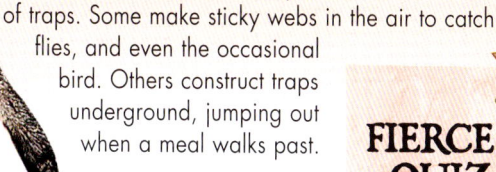

THE STING

Scorpions are close relatives of the spider. Although they live in fewer parts of the world, scorpions kill many more people, usually in self defence. In Mexico, about 1,000 people a year die from scorpion stings. The poison is normally used to help the scorpion kill its next meal.

Mosquito

PERILOUS PEST

The most dangerous insect in the world isn't a predator at all. The mosquito would be a harmless blood-sucking parasite, if it wasn't for the deadly malaria disease that it carries in some parts of the world. About two million people die in Africa each year from mosquito-borne malaria.

FIERCE QUIZ

What size is the biggest spider's web in the world?
a) 1 metre
b) 1.5 metres
c) 2 metres

A garden spider's web contains 30 metres of silk – how much does it weigh?
a) 0.5 mg
b) 1 g
c) 0.5 kg

In scorpion country, what's the first thing you should do every morning?
a) empty out your shoes
b) call for your mum
c) go back to sleep

(answers on page 32)

MAN-EATERS

For all the scary, hungry animals that there are in the world, surprisingly few actually enjoy hunting humans. Most of the large predators of the world have learned that humans can be more trouble than they're worth. But when food is scarce, or the animal is too weak to chase faster prey, humans are back on the menu.

Indo-Chinese tiger

TIGER TROUBLE

Tigers once lived all across southern and eastern Asia, but are now confined to small pockets of suitable territory, squeezed between the spaces humans have taken over for farming and industry. As their supply of prey such as deer and other forest animals runs out, more and more will turn to eating people instead.

JAWS!

Shark attacks on humans are relatively rare, considering their reputation (more people die from bee stings!). Great white sharks are thought to kill about ten people every year, normally in places where seals are plentiful. In these areas, the shark is more likely to confuse divers and surfers for its usual food.

Polar bear

HUNGRY BEAR

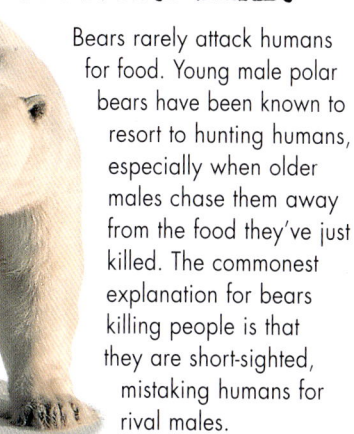

Bears rarely attack humans for food. Young male polar bears have been known to resort to hunting humans, especially when older males chase them away from the food they've just killed. The commonest explanation for bears killing people is that they are short-sighted, mistaking humans for rival males.

THAT'S A LORRY LORRY CROCODILE!

Saltwater crocs have been measured at 7 metres long, but are thought to grow up to 9 metres – that's as long as a lorry!

FIERCE QUIZ

What should you do if you spot a tiger behind you?

a) shout at it
b) climb a tree
c) stare it out

Just before a great white bites, it closes its eyes. Why doesn't it miss?

a) its eyelids are see-through
b) it listens to your muscles
c) its mouth is very big!

Which creature kills most people each year?

a) shark
b) tiger
c) mosquito

(answers on page 32)

QUIZ ANSWERS:

Page 2 b, Hawaiian; c, spots; a, less than 10,000.
Page 5 c, 1 week; a,b,c, trick question – lions lived in all these places in Roman times; b, 15.
Page 7 b, 70-80 kg; c, 64 km/h; b, 4.
Page 9 b, in a burrow; a, make a loud noise; b, 37 cm.
Page 11 c, 9 metres; b, bead-like scales; a, Mexican beaded lizard.
Page 12 c, 2000; c, 7; a, an elephant.
Page 15 a,b,c, trick question – they all have!; b, 10 metres; b, 60 cm.
Page 16 b, send for the antidote; a, Brazil; a, on a leaf.
Page 18 c, 10 metres; b, 225 kg; b, 59-kg impala.
Page 21 c, 9 metres; c, 55 km/h; a, sandpaper.
Page 23 a, 1 kg; c, 300,000 sq metres; a, 40 cm.
Page 25 c, 1,000 kg; c, a brown bear; a, for ingredients for medicines.
Page 26 b, cough them up in pellets; c, peregrine falcon; b, sees its urine.
Page 29 b, 1.5 metres; a, 0.5 mg; a, empty out your shoes.
Page 31 b, climb a tree; b, it listens to your muscles; c, mosquito.

Acknowledgements

We would like to thank Nicola Edwards
and Elizabeth Wiggans for their assistance.
Cartoons by Griff.
Copyright © 1999 *ticktock* Publishing Ltd.
First published in Great Britain by ticktock Publishing Ltd.,
The Offices in the Square, Hadlow, Tonbridge, Kent TN11 0DD, Great Britain.
All rights reserved.
No part of this publication may be reproduced, stored in a retrieval system, or transmitted in any form or by any means electronic, mechanical, photocopying, recording or otherwise, without prior written permission of the copyright owner.
A CIP catalogue record for this book is available from the British Library.

ISBN 1 86007 123 6

Picture Credits: t = top, b = bottom, c = centre, l = left, r=right, OFC = outside front cover, OBC = outside back cover, IFC = inside front cover

Planet Earth Pictures; OFC, 2b, 4, 4/5, 6/7t, 8b, 8/9, 10/11, 11b, 13br, 14/15, 16t, 18/19t, 19c, 20/21, 21br, 22/23, 31c, 30cl. Telegraph Colour Library; 17b, 28/29t. Oxford Scientific Films; IFC & 28/29b, 3, 6b, 15t, 26/27.

Picture research by Image Select. Printed in Hong Kong.